PHONICS PRACTICE Simplified

Book E
Vowel Combinations

Using visual and context clues to learn and practice irregular vowel sounds

IRA/NCTE Standard met for *Phonics Practice Simplified* series

#3: Students apply a wide range of strategies to comprehend, interpret, evaluate, and apppreciate texts. They draw on their prior experience, their interactions with other readers and writers, their knowledge of word meaning and of other texts, their word identification strategies, and their understanding of textual features (for example, sound-letter correspondence, sentence structure, context, graphics).

Cover Design
Elliot Kreloff, Inc.

Essential Learning Products
P.O. Box 2590
Columbus, Ohio 43216-2590

The text and illustrations in this book originally appeared in *Phonics–Vowel Combinations*
©1982 Essential Learning Products
Printed in the United States of America
10 9 8 7 6 5 4 3

PHONICS PRACTICE
Simplified

Vowel Combinations
CONTENTS

Introduction

The purpose of phonics is to help students read new words by sounding them out. The student who uses phonics to decode a word can associate the printed letters with the speech sounds the letters represent and then blend them together to pronounce the word.

There are many vowel sounds that do not follow the rules governing short and long vowels. The purpose of this book, *Vowel Combinations*, is to teach these irregular vowel sounds. Included are the vowel diphthongs, the *r*-controlled vowels, and other irregular vowel combinations.

A *diphthong* is a combination of two vowels, each contributing to the unique sound heard. The vowels in the diphthong *oi*, for instance, do not make the sound of *o* or of *i*, but together form the vowel sound heard in the word *boil*. The diphthongs covered in this book are *oi*, *oy*, *ow*, *ou*, and *ew*.

When a vowel is followed immediately by the letter *r*, its sound is changed. In the word *bird*, for example, the letter *i* has neither the short *i* nor the long *i* sound. There are lessons on *ar*, *er*, *ir*, *or*, and *ur* in this book.

The term *irregular vowels* describes letters or letter combinations, other than diphthongs and *r*-controlled vowels, that do not follow the generalizations of short and long vowels. Irregular vowels included in this book are *oo*, *au*, *aw*, *ea*, *ie*, *ei*, *a* (followed by *l*), and *o* (as in the word *soft*).

Lessons vary in length, depending on difficulty and frequency of occurrence. The lessons include practice in recognizing the vowel sound by using picture clues, rhyming words, and word meanings, and by writing vowels in words and sentences.

The review pages, which occur throughout the book, provide practice in discriminating the sounds of several vowels or vowel combinations.

Vowel Combinations, as well as the other books in this series, is meant for use at home or in school. At home, the books may be used as a supplement to schoolwork. In school, the books may be used as a phonics text in the primary grades or as a supplementary aid for students who need extra help in phonics. Teachers at the junior high or high school levels may also find these books useful for remediation.

oi

When the vowels **oi** blend together, they make the sound you hear in the word **oil.**

Add **oi** to each of these words. Read the words.

s ___ ___ l

p ___ ___ nt

c ___ ___ l

c ___ ___ ns

v ___ ___ ce

___ ___ l

oi

Add **oi** to each of these words. Draw a line from a word in the first column to a word that rhymes with it in the second column.

b ___ ___ l •	• j ___ ___ nt
j ___ ___ n •	• s ___ ___ l
p ___ ___ nt •	• v ___ ___ ce
ch ___ ___ ce •	• c ___ ___ n
m ___ ___ st •	• h ___ ___ st

oi

Add **oi** to each of these words. Read the words to yourself. Write the number of each word next to its meaning.

1. s ___ ___ l	3. m ___ ___ st	5. n ___ ___ se
2. c ___ ___ n	4. b ___ ___ l	6. rej ___ ___ ce

____ wet

____ a sound

____ a piece of metal money

____ dirt

____ to feel happy

____ to bubble when heated

oi

Circle a word to complete each sentence.

1. Wrap the cookies in (foil toil).
2. Do you know what that (spoil noise) is?
3. Use your finger to (point joint) to the letter.
4. I could not hear your (moist voice) on the telephone.
5. Keep the (soil toil) for the plant wet.
6. Would you like to (coin join) our club?

When the vowels **oy** blend together, they make the sound you hear in the word **toy.**

Add **oy** to each of these words. Read the words.

oy

b ___ ___

j ___ ___ ful

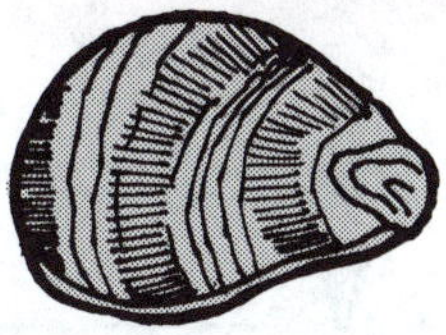

___ ___ ster

v ___ ___ age

t ___ ___ s

cowb ___ ___

oy

Fill in each blank with an **oy** word that rhymes with **enjoy.**

something to play with ____________

a person who ropes steers ____________

a happy feeling ____________

a boy's name ____________

not a girl, but a ____________

Add **oy** to each of these words. Read the words to yourself. Write the number of each word next to its meaning.

oy

1. r ___ ___ al
2. v ___ ___ age
3. ___ ___ ster
4. j ___ ___ ful
5. l ___ ___ al
6. t ___ ___

___ a sea animal with a shell

___ having to do with kings and queens

___ full of joy

___ something to play with

___ faithful

___ to travel by ship

oy

Circle a word to complete each sentence.

1. The (toy boy) truck was painted bright green.
2. The (joyful voyage) lasted for days.
3. The king sat on his (loyal royal) throne.
4. A pearl was found inside the (oyster loyal).
5. Did you (enjoy toy) the movie?
6. The (cowboy oyster) roped a steer.

When the letters **ow** blend together, they sometimes make the sound you hear in the word **now.**
Circle the pictures whose names have the **ow** sound.
Cross out those that do not.

ow

ow

Complete only the words that contain **ow.** Cross out the pictures whose names do not.

t ___ ___ n

cr ___ ___ d

st ___ ___ l

p ___ ___ der

v ___ ___ els

t ___ ___ er

sh ___ ___ er

fr ___ ___ n

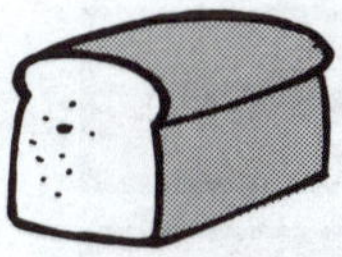
br ___ ___ d

Say the name of each picture to yourself. Then write it.
All the names are **ow** words.

ow

 ______________

 ______________

 ______________

 ______________

 ______________

 ______________

ow

Complete each sentence. Use an **ow** word that rhymes with the word in the box.

down	In this picture, color the road ______________ .
flower	It looks like we will have a rain ______________ .
now	The ______________ is milked early in the morning.
vowel	Wipe your wet hands on this ______________ .
crown	We all laughed at the circus ______________ .
how	We watched the farmer ______________ his field.

When the vowels **ou** blend together, they sometimes make the sound you hear in the word **out.**

ou

Add **ou** to each of these words. Read the words.

p ___ ___ ch

m ___ ___ se

b ___ ___ nce

m ___ ___ ntain

h ___ ___ se

cl ___ ___ d

ou

Add **ou** to each of these words. Draw a line from a word in the first column to a rhyming word in the second column.

r ___ ___ nd •	• m ___ ___ th
s ___ ___ th •	• ab ___ ___ t
h ___ ___ se •	• s ___ ___ nd
sh ___ ___ t •	• c ___ ___ ch
pr ___ ___ d •	• m ___ ___ se
p ___ ___ ch •	• l ___ ___ d

Add **ou** to each of these words. Read the words to yourself. Write the number of each word next to its meaning.

ou

1. gr ___ ___ nd
2. h ___ ___ r
3. h ___ ___ nd
4. ___ ___ t
5. sh ___ ___ t
6. p ___ ___ nd

____ a dog

____ sixty minutes

____ to call in a loud voice

____ the earth

____ to hit or beat

____ opposite of "in"

ou

Circle a word to complete each sentence.

1. The boy (found sound) the book he had lost.
2. Can you (count cloud) this money for me?
3. Do you know what this story is (shout about)?
4. Our (mouse house) needs painting this year.
5. Will you sit at the (round pound) table?
6. Plant these seeds in the (ground mouth).

ou

Sometimes the vowels **ou** make the sound of short **u** as in **touch**. Add **ou** to each of these words. Read the words.

en ___ ___ gh

c ___ ___ ntry

r ___ ___ gh

tr ___ ___ ble

d ___ ___ ble

t ___ ___ gh

c ___ ___ ple

c ___ ___ sin

ew

When the letters **ew** blend together, they make the sound you hear in the word **new.**

Complete only the words that have the **ew** sound. Cross out the pictures whose names do not.

scr ___ ___

st ___ ___

j ___ ___ els

c ___ ___

fl ___ ___

h ___ ___ se

Fill in each blank with an **ew** word that rhymes with **blew.**

ew

to bite and grind with your teeth ____________

not very many ____________

opposite of “old” ____________

little drops of water that form at night ____________

the persons who run a ship or plane ____________

the sound a cat makes ____________

ew

Circle a word to complete each sentence.

1. Every child (knew few) the answer.
2. She (chew threw) the ball over the fence.
3. The flower (dew grew) to be 12 inches tall.
4. The class (drew crew) pictures for the contest.
5. The strong winds (brew blew) the tree down.
6. The bird (flew few) to the highest branch.

REVIEW

Say the name of each picture to yourself. Circle the letters that spell its vowel sound.

oi ow

ou ew

ow oi

oi ew

ou oy

oy ou

REVIEW

Say the name of each picture to yourself. Write **oi, oy, ow, ou,** or **ew** to complete its name.

___ ___ster

cl ___ ___ n

___ ___ l

m ___ ___ ntain

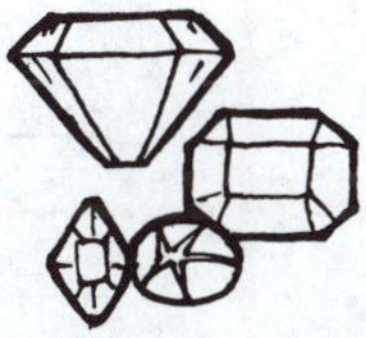

j ___ ___ els

fl ___ ___ er

REVIEW

Complete the word in each sentence by writing **oi, oy, ow, ou,** or **ew** in the blank.

1. The child thr ____ ____ the ball high in the air.
2. What kind of fl ____ ____ ers grow in your garden?
3. Would you like to take a v ____ ____ age across the ocean?
4. The p ____ ____ nt on my pencil broke.
5. Use a hammer to p ____ ____ nd the nail into the wood.

REVIEW

Build **oi** and **ow** words. Read each meaning. Add a beginning consonant or consonant blend to complete each word.

____	oil	to cook	____	own	opposite of "up"
____	oil	tin paper	____	own	a small city
____	oil	dirt	____ ____	own	a color
____	oil	to wind up	____ ____	own	a king's hat
____ ____	oil	to ruin	____ ____	own	a worried look

ar

Complete only the words that contain the **ar** sound as in the word **car.** Cross out the pictures whose names do not.

st ___ ___

j ___ ___

m ___ ___ key

c ___ ___

s ___ ___ t

y ___ ___ n

b ___ ___ l

c ___ ___ t

___ ___ m

ar

Complete each sentence. Use an **ar** word that rhymes with the word in the box.

car	How __________ is it to the next city?
mark	It is very __________ inside this closet.
hard	Did you send her a birthday __________ ?
parted	Has the show __________ yet?
harm	I hear the fire __________ !
Marty	Would you like to come to my __________ ?

ar

Write **ar** in each set of blanks to complete the word. Read the words to yourself. Draw a line from each word to its meaning.

c ___ ___ ●	● begin
m ___ ___ ket ●	● an automobile
st ___ ___ t ●	● not dull
m ___ ___ ch ●	● opposite of "near"
sh ___ ___ p ●	● to walk like a soldier
f ___ ___ ●	● a store

ar

Say the name of each picture to yourself. Then write it. All the names are **ar** words.

 ______________

 ______________

 ______________

 ______________

 ______________

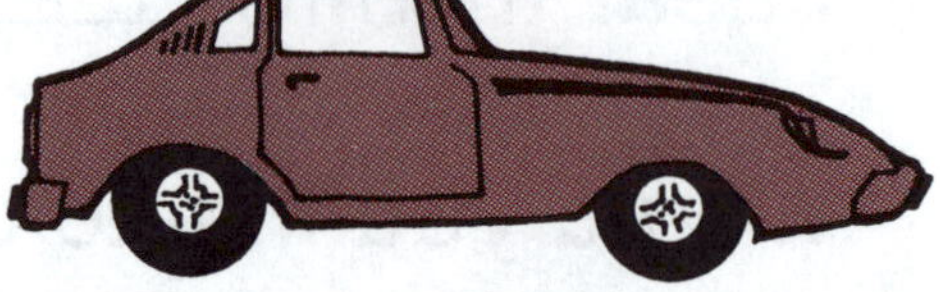 ______________

er

Complete only the words that contain the **er** sound as in the word **her.** Cross out the pictures whose names do not.

f ___ ___ n

barb ___ ___

spid ___ ___

___ ___ l

p ___ ___ son

m ___ ___ se

lett ___ ___

f ___ ___ e

h ___ ___ d

er

Write **er** in each set of blanks to complete the word. Read the words to yourself. Draw a line from each word to its meaning.

silv ___ ___ •	• a large stream
g ___ ___ m •	• a shiny metal
riv ___ ___ •	• opposite of "him"
p ___ ___ ch •	• a green plant
h ___ ___ •	• this makes you sick
f ___ ___ n •	• what a bird sits on

er

Fill in the blanks to make a word that is the opposite of the word next to it.

___ er   him

___ ___ ___ er   before

___ ___ ___ ___ er   brother

___ ___ ___ ___ er   mother

___ ___ er   under

___ ___ ___ ___ er   summer

er

Say the name of each picture to yourself. Then write it. All the names are **er** words.

 ____________

 ____________

 ____________

____

 ____________

 ____________

Complete only the words that contain the **ir** sound as in the word **bird.** Cross out the pictures whose names do not.

ir

g ___ ___ l

b ___ ___

d ___ ___ t

f ___ ___ h

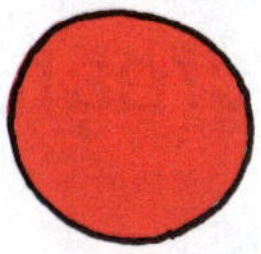

c ___ ___ cle

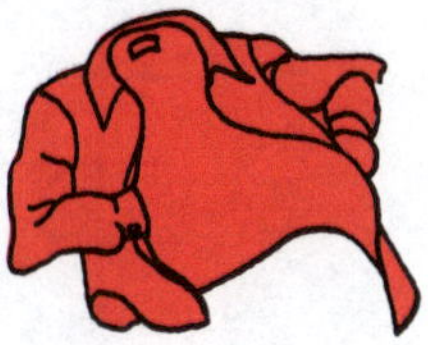

sh ___ ___ t

st ___ ___

th ___ ___ d

y ___ ___ n

ir

Write **ir** in each set of blanks to complete the word. Read the words to yourself. Draw a line from each word to its meaning.

th ___ ___ sty ●	● to wiggle around
ch ___ ___ p ●	● the sound a bird makes
f ___ ___ ●	● wanting a drink
squ ___ ___ m ●	● a man
f ___ ___ st ●	● a kind of tree
s ___ ___ ●	● number one

Fill in the blanks to make a word. The meaning of the word is next to it.

ir

___ ___ ir	to mix something
___ ir	what you would call a man
___ ir ___	a creature with feathers
___ ___ ir ___	girl's clothing
___ ir ___	soil
___ ___ ir ___	after "second"

ir

Say the name of each picture to yourself. Then write it. All the names are **ir** words.

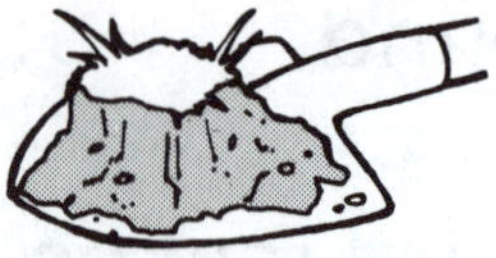

____

____

____

____

____

____

Complete only the words that contain the **or** sound as in the word **for.** Cross out the pictures whose names do not.

or

th ____ ____ n

c ____ ____ n

st ____ ____ m

c ____ ____ k

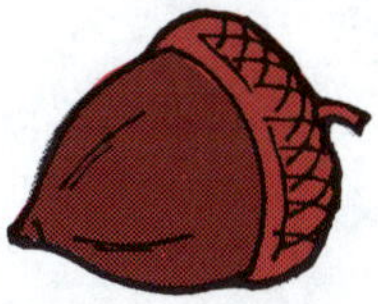

ac ____ ____ n

n ____ ____ th

cl ____ ____ d

sw ____ ____ d

m ____ ____ th

or

Write **or** in each set of blanks to complete the word. Read the words to yourself. Draw a line from each word to its meaning.

st ____ ____ m ●	● meat from a pig
p ____ ____ k ●	● opposite of "tall"
th ____ ____ n ●	● bad weather
sh ____ ____ t ●	● a sharp point on a plant
st ____ ____ e ●	● one more than thirty-nine
f ____ ____ ty ●	● a place to buy things

Say the name of each picture to yourself. Then write it.
All the names are **or** words.

or

 ____________

 ____________

 ____________

 ____________

____

 ____________

or

Complete each sentence. Use an **or** word that rhymes with the word in the box.

torn	In what month were you ____________ ?
fork	We are having a ____________ roast for dinner.
short	What ____________ do you like to play?
torch	Our front ____________ needs a coat of paint.
wore	I need to buy some bread at the ____________ .
cord	The knight killed the dragon with a ____________ .

or

Sometimes the letters **or** make the sound of **er** as in the word **work**. Add **or** to each of these words. Read the words.

col ___ ___

doct ___ ___

fav ___ ___

maj ___ ___

neighb ___ ___

w ___ ___ ld

w ___ ___ m

w ___ ___ k

may ___ ___

w ___ ___ d

or

Circle a word to complete each sentence.

1. There are many people living in the (word world).
2. A (doctor major) helps to heal the sick.
3. What is your favorite (color favor)?
4. We watched the (word worm) crawl in the soil.
5. The (mayor favor) of the city gave a speech.
6. Do you know all your (neighbors majors)?

Complete only the words that contain the **ur** sound as in the word **hurt.** Cross out the pictures whose names do not.

ur

ch ___ ___ ch

ch ___ ___ r

t ___ ___ tle

b ___ ___ k

p ___ ___ se

sp ___ ___

t ___ ___ key

cr ___ ___

n ___ ___ se

ur

Write **ur** in each set of blanks to complete the word. Read the words to yourself. Draw a line from each word to its meaning.

p ___ ___ ple ●	● an animal with a shell
t ___ ___ n ●	● to explode
b ___ ___ st ●	● to damage by fire
t ___ ___ tle ●	● a violet color
b ___ ___ n ●	● the hair of an animal
f ___ ___ ●	● to twist

Fill in the blanks to make a word. The meaning of the word is next to it.

ur

___ ur ___ ___	a pocketbook
___ ur	the soft hair on a cat
___ ur ___	edge of the sidewalk
___ ur ___	to cause pain
___ ur ___	the sound of a happy cat
___ ur ___ ___	one who cares for the sick

ur

Say the name of each picture to yourself. Then write it. All the names are **ur** words.

____

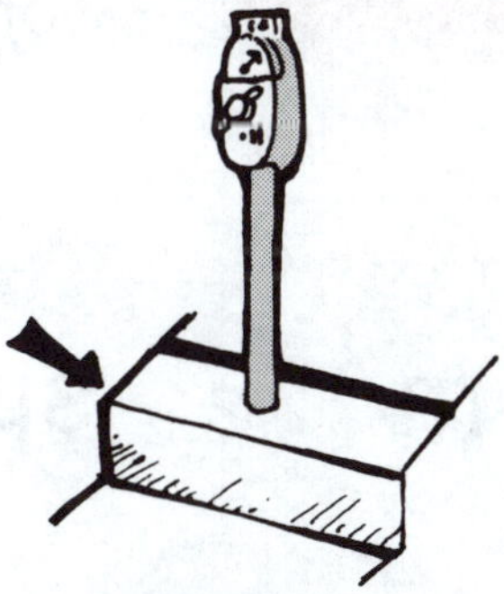

____

____

____

____

____

REVIEW

Read each word to yourself. Draw a line from each word to its picture.

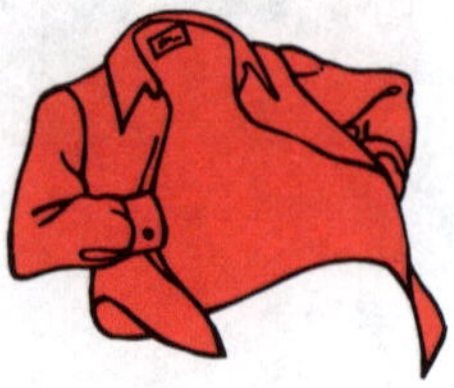

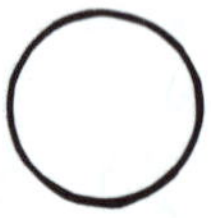

shark
fern
shirt
horn
turtle
person
forty
circle
star
church

REVIEW

Complete each word with **ar, er, ir, or,** or **ur.** Read the words to yourself.

____ ____ m	sp ____ ____ k	th ____ ____ d
h ____ ____	wh ____ ____ l	s ____ ____ ve
sk ____ ____ t	ch ____ ____ ch	g ____ ____ den
h ____ ____ n	st ____ ____ m	n ____ ____ se
h ____ ____ t	patt ____ ____ n	ac ____ ____ n

REVIEW

Say the name of each picture to yourself. Write **ar, er, ir, or,** or **ur** to complete its name.

sh ___ ___ k

p ___ ___ se

sk ___ ___ t

c ___ ___ cle

lett ___ ___

d ___ ___ t

f ___ ___ ty

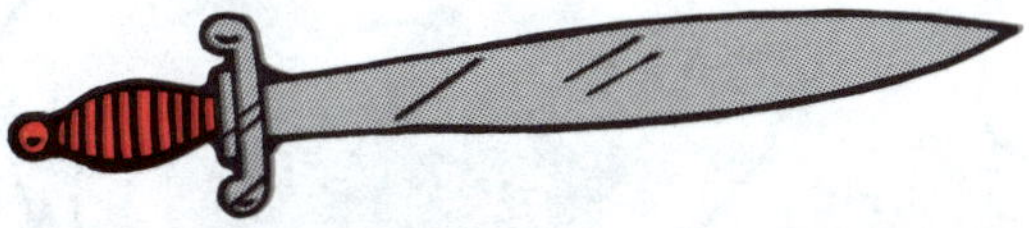

sw ___ ___ d

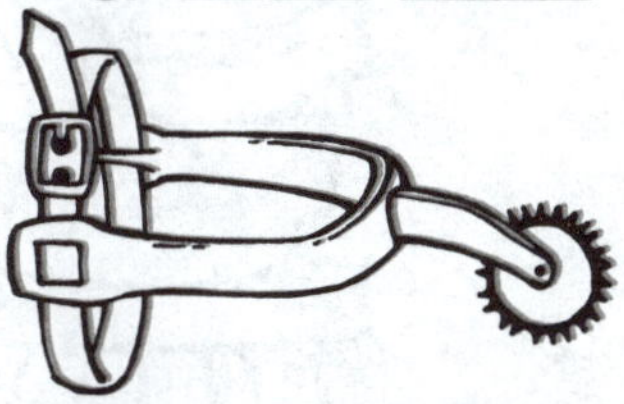

sp ___ ___

REVIEW

Circle a word to complete each sentence.

1. Did you (turn burn fern) your finger?
2. We visited an old (for fork fort).
3. Two horses were pulling the (car card cart).
4. We had to (park part dart) the car around the corner.
5. This is the (herd third bird) home run you hit.
6. The bird was sitting on its (perch church birth).

The vowels **oo** sometimes make the sound you hear in the word **boot.** This is the sound of long **oo.** Circle four or more things in the picture that have the long **oo** sound.

OO

Complete each sentence. Use a long **oo** word that rhymes with the word in the box.

oo

root	Linda will ____________ the arrow at the target.
mood	What ____________ shall we take for our picnic?
loop	Al trained his dog to jump through a ____________ .
fool	Let's take a swim in the ____________ .
soon	We shall eat our lunch at ____________ .
room	A new ____________ sweeps clean.

oo

Fill in the blanks to make a word. The meaning of the word is next to it.

___ oo ___	not hot
___ oo ___	what you eat
___ oo ___ ___	one of your teeth
___ oo ___ ___	an animal with antlers
___ ___ ___ oo ___	a place where you learn
___ oo ___	a part of a plant

Say the name of each picture to yourself. Then write it.
All the names are **oo** words.

oo

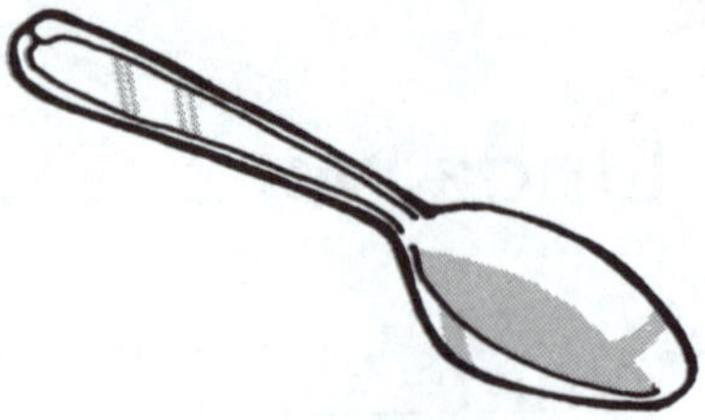

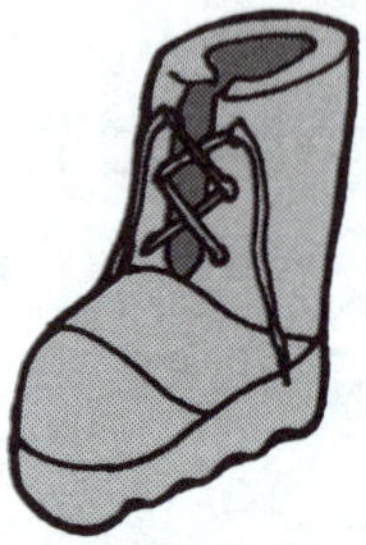

oo

The vowels **oo** sometimes make the sound you hear in the word **foot.** This is the sound of short **oo.** Circle four or more things in the picture that have the short **oo** sound.

Write **oo** in each set of blanks to complete the word. Read the words to yourself. Draw a line from each word to its meaning.

oo

b ___ ___ k ●	● what you read
f ___ ___ t ●	● from a tree
w ___ ___ d ●	● a small stream
h ___ ___ k ●	● 12 inches
br ___ ___ k ●	● what you use to catch a fish
s ___ ___ t ●	● dirt

oo

Complete each sentence. Use a short **oo** word that rhymes with the word in the box.

took	__________ at the hawks!
goods	The Scouts camped out in the __________ .
hood	He __________ on a chair to reach the shelf.
book	The ground __________ when the train went by.
wood	Today was a __________ day.
foot	The chimney was full of __________ .

Say the name of each picture to yourself. Then write it.
All the names are **oo** words.

oo

 ______________

 ______________

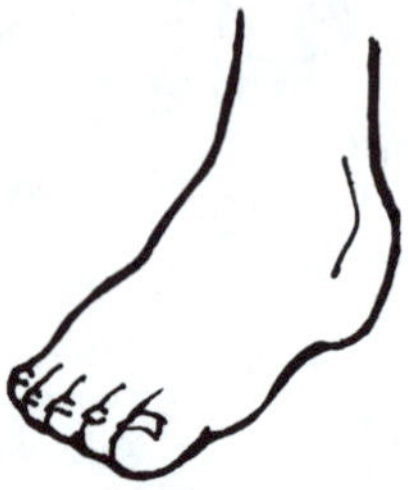 ______________

 ______________

 ______________

 ______________

REVIEW

Read each word to yourself. Draw a line from each word to its picture.

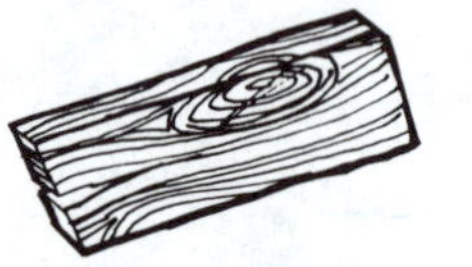

spoon
hook
wood
rooster
stool
hood
moon
book
food
cook

REVIEW

Say each word to yourself. Draw a line from each word to its vowel sound.

loose		soon
crook	**long oo**	cool
tooth		foot
smooth	**short oo**	brook
hook		room

REVIEW

Circle the words that contain **oo**. Above each **oo** word, write **long** or **short** to show how the **oo** is pronounced.

1. The school cooks good food.

2. We took the moose from the zoo to the woods.

3. He stood on the roof and looked at the moon.

4. I am in the mood to choose a book on soot.

au

The vowels **au** usually make the sound you hear in **caught.** Complete only the words that have the **au** sound. Cross out the pictures whose names do not.

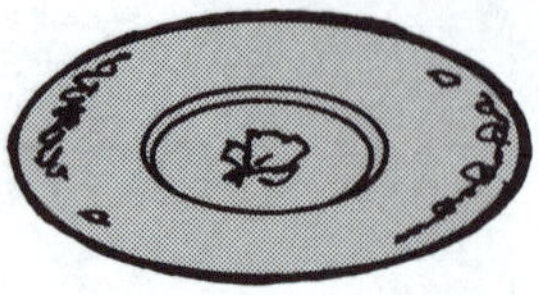

s ____ ____ cer

____ ____ to

s ____ ____ sage

ch ____ ____ ch

f ____ ____ cet

____ ____ tumn

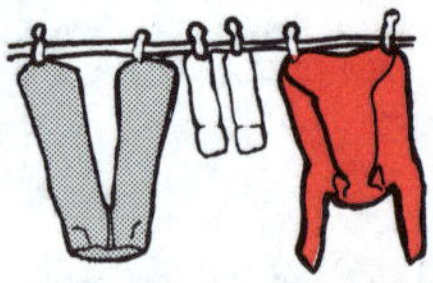

l ____ ____ ndry

f ____ ____ e

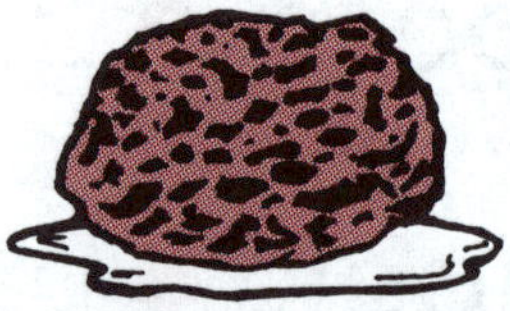

sp ____ ____ ge

au

Write **au** in each set of blanks to complete the word. Read the words to yourself. Draw a line from each word to its meaning.

f ____ ____ lt	full of ghosts
h ____ ____ nted	carry
____ ____ tumn	blame
h ____ ____ l	plate under a cup
d ____ ____ ghter	the fall season
s ____ ____ cer	Dad and Mother's girl

Fill in the blanks to make words that match each meaning.

au

___ au ___ ___ ___ past of "catch"

___ au ___ ___ ___ a little plate that goes under a cup

au ___ ___ ___ ___ ___ ___ ___ ___ a car

___ au ___ ___ ___ a water spout

au ___ ___ ___ ___ September, October, and November

___ au ___ ___ ___ ___ where you wash clothes

aw

The letters **aw** usually make the sound you hear in **yawn.** Complete only the words that have the **aw** sound. Cross out the pictures whose names do not.

p ___ ___

str ___ ___

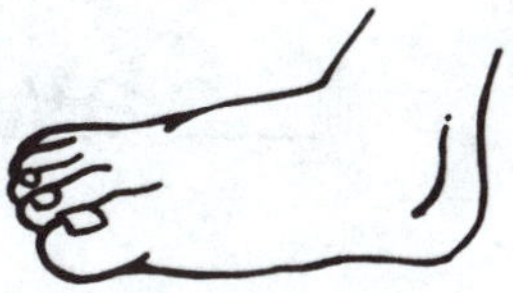

f ___ ___ t

h ___ ___ se

s ___ ___

sh ___ ___ l

h ___ ___ k

l ___ ___ n

r ___ ___

Complete each sentence. Write a word that ends with **aw** in each blank.

aw

1. From the top of the cliff, we ___ ___ ___ the entire town.

2. Can you ___ ___ ___ ___ a picture of an elephant?

3. Take the meat out of the freezer to ___ ___ ___ ___.

4. It is against the ___ ___ ___ to park there.

5. May I have a ___ ___ ___ ___ ___ for my milk?

6. We like ___ ___ ___ carrots better than cooked ones.

aw

Fill in the blanks to make a word. The meaning of the word is next to it.

___ aw ___	to open your mouth wide
___ ___ aw	a cat's fingernail
___ aw ___	sunrise
___ aw ___	a grassy yard
___ aw ___	a bird with sharp claws
___ ___ aw	to melt

REVIEW

he **aw** sound may be spelled **aw** or **au.** Say the name of ach picture to yourself. Write **aw** or **au** in the blanks to omplete each word.

 f ___ ___ cet

 p ___ ___

 h ___ ___ k

 s ___ ___ sage

 s ___ ___

 sh ___ ___ l

 ___ ___ to

 str ___ ___

 l ___ ___ n

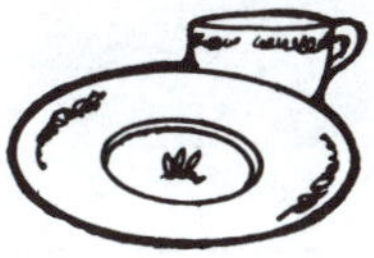 s ___ ___ cer

REVIEW

Draw a circle around the name of each picture.

 sausage laundry autumn	 paw hawk saw	 faucet taught auto
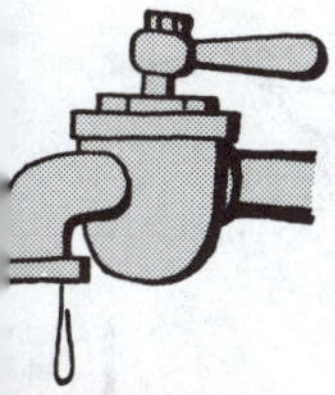 faucet fault daughter	 caught autumn saucer	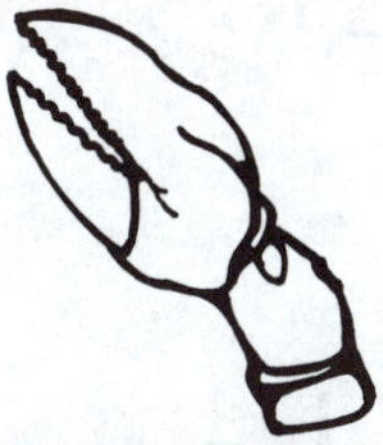 straw claw shawl
 saucer faucet sausage	 straw shawl claw	 lawn yawn claw

REVIEW

Each of these words can be completed by adding **au** or **aw.** Fill in the blanks with the correct letter combinations.

l ___ ___ ndry   str ___ ___ berry   r ___ ___

dr ___ ___   cl ___ ___   c ___ ___ ght

h ___ ___ nted   h ___ ___ l   d ___ ___ ghte

f ___ ___ lt   th ___ ___   l ___ ___ n

y ___ ___ n   ___ ___ tumn   l ___ ___

al

When **a** is followed by **l,** it usually makes the **aw** sound. Complete only the words that contain **al.** Cross out the pictures whose names do not.

w ___ ___ k

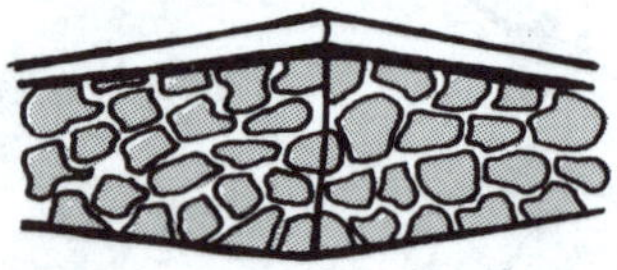
w ___ ___ l

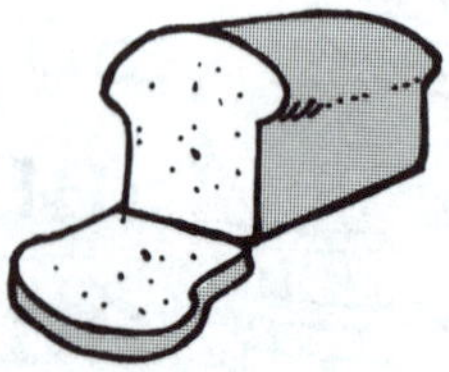
br ___ ___ c

b ___ ___ l

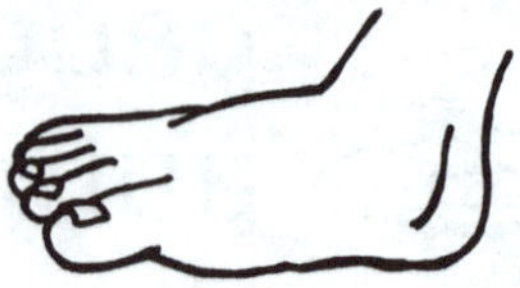
f ___ ___ t

f ___ ___ l

h ___ ___ l

s ___ ___ t

cr ___ ___ r

Write **al** in each set of blanks to complete the word. Read the words to yourself. Draw a line from each word to its meaning.

al

t ___ ___ k ●	● everything
h ___ ___ t ●	● forever
w ___ ___ k ●	● stop
___ ___ ways ●	● to travel by foot
___ ___ l ●	● little
sm ___ ___ l ●	● to speak

al

Complete each sentence. Use a word that rhymes with the word in the box.

talk	Do you __________ to school each day?
halt	This meat needs some __________ .
ball	Did someone __________ me on the phone?
hall	Help me hang these pictures on the __________ .
small	The basketball players are very __________ .
all	The leaves will begin to __________ off the trees.

Sometimes the vowel **o** makes the sound of **aw** as in the word **frog.** Complete only the words that have the **aw** sound spelled with an **o.** Cross out the pictures whose names do not.

d ___ g

f ___ sh

fr ___ g

j ___ r

l ___ g

cr ___ ss

m ___ th

b ___ rd

h ___ g

Fill in the blanks to make a word that is the opposite of the word next to it.

o ___ ___ on

___ o ___ ___ short

___ ___ o ___ ___ right

___ o ___ ___ found

___ o ___ ___ loud

___ ___ ___ o ___ ___ weak

Sometimes the vowel **o** makes the sound of short **u** as in the word **of**. Write **o** in each blank to complete the words. Read the words. Draw a line from each word to its meaning.

o

m ___ ther	not anything
n ___ thing	about 30 days
s ___ me	Mom
m ___ nth	clothing for the hand
c ___ me	a few
gl ___ ve	to arrive

REVIEW

Say each word to yourself. Draw a line from each word to the box that shows how the **o** is pronounced.

song		son
some	**aw**	belong
across		nothing
of	**u**	other
broth		loss

ea

Sometimes the vowels **ea** make the sound of short **e** as in the word **dead.** Complete only the words that have the short **e** sound spelled with **ea.** Cross out the pictures whose names do not.

h ___ ___ d

sn ___ ___

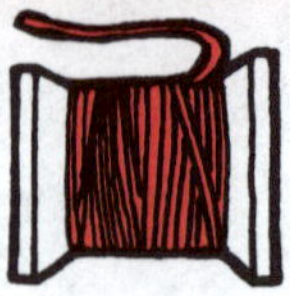

thr ___ ___ d

al ___ ___ m

h ___ ___ vy

br ___ ___ th

f ___ ___ ther

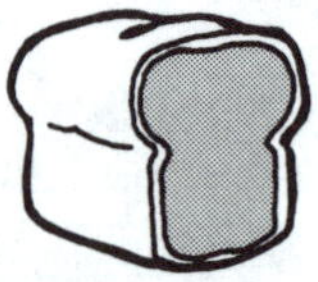

br ___ ___ d

___ ___ ght

ea

Fill in the blanks to make a word. The meaning of the word is next to it.

___ ea ___	not living
___ ea ___	top part of the body
___ ___ ea ___	part of a sandwich
___ ea ___ ___ ___	opposite of "sickness"
___ ea ___ ___ ___ ___	rain, snow, sun
___ ea ___	a heavy, soft metal

Circle a word to complete each sentence.

ea

1. (Spread Bread) jam on my toast.
2. Have you (read dead) a good book lately?
3. I choose this kite (instead breath) of that one.
4. My pencil (head lead) broke.
5. Will you (feather thread) the needle for me?
6. The box is very (health heavy).

ie

Sometimes the vowels **ie** make the sound of long **e** as in the word **chief.** Complete only the words that have the long **e** sound spelled with **ie.** Cross out the pictures whose names do not.

ch ___ ___ f

___ ___ l

sh ___ ___ ld

fr ___ ___ t

p ___ ___ ce

thr ___ ___ d

h ___ ___ se

f ___ ___ ld

Write **ie** in each set of blanks to complete the word. Read the words to yourself. Draw a line from each word to its meaning.

ie

gr ___ ___ f •
bel ___ ___ ve •
p ___ ___ ce •
ch ___ ___ f •
shr ___ ___ k •

• a leader
• sadness
• to have faith in
• to scream
• a part of something

ei

Sometimes the vowels **ei** make the sound of long **a** as in the word **freight.** Complete only the words that have the long **a** sound spelled with **ei.** Cross out the pictures whose names do not.

sl ___ ___ gh

___ ___ ght

cr ___ ___ n

v ___ ___ l

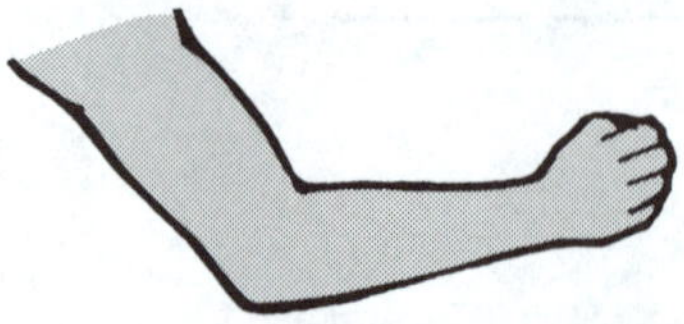
___ ___ m

w ___ ___ gh

r ___ ___ ndeer

n ___ ___ ghbors

f ___ ___ ther

Write a word for each meaning. The word will sound like the word in the box but will be spelled with the letters **ei**.

ei

six plus two	______________	ate
put something on a scale	______________	way
a blood vessel	______________	vane
what a horse says	______________	nay
what you hold when riding a horse	______________	rains

REVIEW

Say the name of each picture to yourself. Then write it. All the words contain **ar, er, ir, or,** or **ur.**

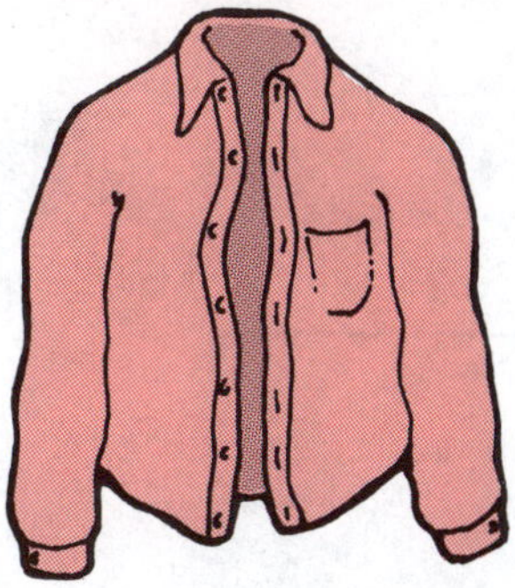
____

____

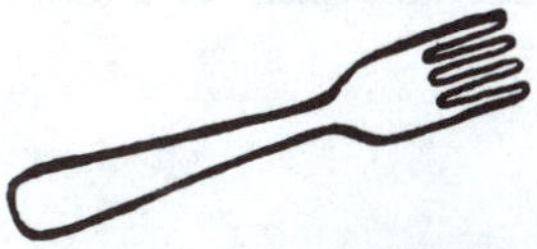
____

40
____

____

____

REVIEW

The **oy** sound can be spelled **oi** or **oy**. Fill in the blanks with **oi** or **oy** to make words that match each meaning.

___ ___ l	a greasy liquid
r ___ ___ al	belonging to the king
c ___ ___ n	a piece of money
enj ___ ___	to have a good time
t ___ ___	something you play with
s ___ ___ l	earth

REVIEW

The **ou** sound may be spelled **ou** or **ow.** Say the name each picture to yourself. Write **ou** or **ow** in the blanks complete each word.

 m ___ ___ th

 c ___ ___

 ___ ___ l

 c ___ ___ ch

 cr ___ ___ n

 fl ___ ___ er

 m ___ ___ se

 m ___ ___ ntai

The sound of long **oo** may be spelled with **u, oo, ou,** or **ew.** Fill in the blanks with **u, oo, ou,** or **ew** to make a word. It should be the opposite of the word next to it.

oo

____ ____ se tight

____ ____ me

____ ____ l warm

____ ____ ner later

____ ____ old

____ ge tiny

REVIEW

The **aw** sound may be spelled **a, al, aw, au,** or **o.** Fill in the blanks with **a, al, aw, au,** or **o** to make words that match each meaning.

w ____ sh to clean with water

____ ____ ways forever

p ____ ____ a dog's foot

r ____ ____ not cooked

s ____ ____ ce what goes on spaghetti

s ____ ng something you sing

REVIEW

Circle the word in each row that sounds the same as the first word.

piece	pace	pack	peace	peach
some	sum	soap	comb	soon
eight	ache	ate	eat	each
rough	ray	row	ruff	roof
breaks	bears	brakes	barks	bricks
son	song	sign	sun	some

REVIEW

Read these words to yourself. Think of the vowel sour made by the underlined letters. Draw a line from eac word in the first column to a word in the second colum whose vowel sound is the same.

eight •	• zoo
raw •	• boy
chew •	• name
proud •	• auto
curb •	• birch
point •	• down